# 故宮勝縣

## THE NATIONAL PALACE MUSEUM IN PHOTOGRAPHS

國立故宮博物院
**National Palace Museum**

# 序

　　故宮博物院，自民國五十四年在台北外雙溪開館以來，已歷二十一週年。由於社會安定、經濟繁榮、教育普及、加上觀光事業發達，為因應此客觀條件之需要，本院建築、設備、展出方式，歷年來亦多所更新。

　　建築方面從最早仿照「辟雍」的方形四層樓建築，擴建為長方形，復由長方形左右兩翼向前伸展，並添建兩道拱橋，成為目前形式。屋頂由單一的翼樓，而增置左右二座插雲小閣，目前之屋頂有五座大小相間的同樣建築，成為節奏起伏，賓主得宜之配置。由於慶祝建院六十週年，擴建行政大樓，使原來一樓辦公室全部改換為展示室，展出空間又增加了三分之一強。正廳頂樓之翼樓，復布置為「三希堂」陳設展示及古典茶藝雅座，便利觀眾於游觀之餘，得以片刻茶熟香溫之憩息。

　　中華文物，實為中華民族德慧智術之反映，而其培養又多得之天人合一——自然——之思想，故中國文學起源甚早。書畫之境界，亦多契合自然之境界。右軍之蘭亭修禊，東坡之赤壁夜遊，王銑之西園雅集，皆此中之最著者。故宮既為人文薈萃之地，不可無林園勝景以為襯託，此為「至善園」營建之動機。園中亭台不作明、清雕樑畫棟之彩繪，而以宋、明之雅素為依歸。碧橋水榭，加以流觴曲水、竹樹蔥鬱，亦頗足以遣懷而見會心。

　　過去故宮出版，素以文物為主，對於院內院外之景觀，尚少置意。攝影名家董敏先生，與故宮淵源頗深，曾任故宮文物事業攝影，對故宮二十年來之興革變遷，瞭若指掌。發心拍攝「故宮勝槩」專集，其資料收集之精到，畫面角度取景之優美，有出人意表者。如「故宮之成長——二十年來之擴建工程」，將本院歷年擴建之歷程，甚至新舊倉庫之今昔，一一列舉眼前，足可見其用心之深而且細。

　　「至善園」與「後樂園」，為本院提供遊客憩息心神之場地，第一次有系統的，用精美的藝術圖片表而出之，既可供遊客存念，又為未能即臨故宮人士提供臥遊之資料，實富有多重意義。

　　為使本書成為不僅是可看的畫集，而且亦有其可讀處，特商請名作家張曉風女士，為各圖片配置適當之詩詞。詩詞雖錄自古今名句，與圖片內容渾然一體，超越了一般攝影畫集之範圍，使本書生色不少，本院林恭祖先生也為本書配了不少詩文，於此一併致謝。

中華民國七十五年十月三十一日秦孝儀序

**Preface:**

The National Palace Museum first moved to Waishuanghsi, a northern suburb of Taipei, in 1965. During the 21 years since then, the museum has seen numerous changes in its buildings and grounds, in its facilities and in its presentation of exhibits. These changes have been prompted by the dramatic rise in the numbers of domestic and overseas visitors to the museum which has resulted from the development of tourism to the ROC and from the rising educational standards and growing economic prosperity which we enjoy within our own relatively stable society in Taiwan.

The museum's Exhibition block started out as a classic square four-storey building. This was first extended into an oblong, then two wings were added projecting forwards at either end, and finally the block took its present form with the addition to the wings of two samll buildings connected to the Exhibition block by gently curving archways. The roofline of the Exhibition block was extended from a single central roof-ridge to include a pair of smaller square rooftop towers above the left and right wings, and now consists of five rooftop structures of varying size disposed in a pleasing arrangement in which the roofline rises and falls with rhythmic grace. With the addition of the new Administrative block, begun in 1981, the ground floor of the Exhibition block, originally occupied by museum offices, was turned over to further exhibition galleries, expanding the available exhibition area by one third. Meanwhile the central rooftop gallery above the Exhibition block was refitted as a traditional Chinese tearoom, the San Hsi T'ang, incorporating an exhibition of reproductions based on furnishings from a private study of the Ch'ien-lung Emperor. Here visitors may relax from touring the galleries for a few moments over a refreshing pot of fragrant China tea.

The material legacy of Chinese culture reflects the gifted skills of the Chinese people, nurtured largely in the concept that heaven and man share a fundamental oneness, in other words, the idea of Nature. Chinese calligraphy and painting, with their roots in the ancient past, also for the most part enshrine this concept of Nature. Perhaps the most famous cultural expressions of this ethic are to be found in such episodes as Wang Hsi-chih attending the ceremony of springtime purification at the Orchid Pavilion, Su Tung-p'o making a nocturnal boat trip to view the scenery of Red Cliff, and Wang Hsien's gathering of literary aesthetes in the Western Garden. In its role as a focal point of Chinese culture the National Palace Museum could hardly be without its own gardens and scenic panoramas to provide a suitably attractive setting, and such was the motive behind the construction within the museum grounds of the Chih-shan Garden. The garden's pavilions and other buildings are not decorated with the gaudy paintwork associated with the later imperial period of the Ming and Ch'ing dynasties, but rather look back to the unadorned style of the earlier Sung, Yuan and early Ming dynasties. Here Green Bridge waterside pavilion looks out over the winding Stream of Floating Goblets, and everywhere the garden with its leafy trees and shady bamboos provides an atmosphere conducive to private relaxation and a pleasing sense of intimacy.

Past publications of the museum have been concerned primarily with the museum's collection as such, and scant attention has been paid as yet to more general views of the museum's exhibition galleries, external aspect and surrounding grounds. In remedying this, we are fortunate to have had the services of Mr. Tung Min, a distinguished photographic artist who has enjoyed a long association with the National Palace Museum, and who in his capacity as staff photographer of the museum's collection has experienced at first hand all the many alterations and improvements at the museum over the past two decades. In preparing this edition of "The National Palace Museum in Photographs" he has shown extraordinary thoroughness in assembling his materials and in devising eye-catching views and picturesque camera angles. For instance, in the section entitled "The Growth of the National Palace Museum — expansion work over the past 20 years" he illustrates every stage in the museum's growth in recent years, even down to changes in the storage vaults. This may be thought sufficient proof of how well thought-out and meticulous an approach he has adopted towards his task.

4

The Chih-shan Garden and the museum's rear garden are areas provided by the museum by way of rest and relaxation for our visitors. Now for the first time these gardens are systematically illustrated in a collection of fine artistic photographs which may either be kept by visitors as a memento, or can allow those who have not yet had the chance to visit the museum to gain a vivid impression of its surroundings.

In order to make this book something more than simply a set of pictures to admire, and to give it a more piquant appeal to the reader, we asked the distinguished authoress Ms. Chang Hsiao-feng to append suitable extracts from Chinese poetry to various of the photographs. These extracts, taken from poetry ranging from ancient times up to the present day, blend into one with the pictures they accompany, and help bring the book to life in a way which lifts it above the scope of more run-of-the-mill photographic essays. Mr. Lin Kung-tsu of the museum staff also supplied several more verse quotations by way of captions, and to both of these as well as to our photographer I would like to take this opportunity of expressing my most sincere thanks.

Ch'in Hsiao-i, Director
31 October, 1986

# 故宮勝覽

## 目 錄

# THE NATIONAL PALACE MUSEUM
# IN PHOTOGRAPHS

## CONTENTS

如跂斯翼，如矢斯棘，如鳥斯革，如翼斯飛。

（詩　小雅　斯干篇）

"Reverently rising on tiptoe, swift as an arrow, Spreading his wings like a pheasant taking flight — Thus is the lord where he ascends." — *Classic of Odes*, Chou Dynasty (11th century-256 B.C.)

迎賓大道側望

Side view of the entrance walkway.

結伴往來，高談古今。
"Strolling in small groups. Discussing lofty matters past and present".

廣場前的迎賓大道
Entrance walkway and forecourt.

勝地初相引，徐徐得自娛 。
　　　　　　　（唐　杜甫詩）
"Where scenic beauty draws you,
First pleasures grow with leisured
contemplation." — Tu Fu, T'ang
Dynasty (618-907)

奈何四海盡滔滔，湛然一境平如砥。
（唐 韋莊詩）

"All rivers flow at last into the sea. Whose clear depths form a serenely calm expanse." — Wei Chuang, T'ang Dynasty (618-907)

本院廣場前「天下爲公」牌坊遠景
View of the inscription "The World is our Common Heritage" in front of the museum forecourt.

有朋自遠方來，不亦樂乎。
"How joyful when friends arrive
from afar."

廣場前的重階
Steps leading up
to the forecourt.

童稚化的守門銅獅
Bronze guardian lions
at the main entrance.

廻升天地外，豁見天地心。
（唐　李幼卿詩）
"Wafting far beyond earth and sky, The world's true meaning grows immediately apparent." — Li Yu-ch'ing, T'ang Dynasty (618-907)

捍衛中國文化的　先總統蔣公銅像
Bronze statue of the late President Chiang Kai-shek, a great guardian of Chinese culture.

青山影裏古今人　（唐　高麗詩人　崔致遠詩）
"Here in the shade of green-clad hillsides gather scholars
who breathe life into the past." — Ts'ui Chih-yuan,
T'ang Dynasty (618-907)

故宮院前廣場與新館
Museum forecourt and
new administration &
research block.

樓角臨風廻，椰林蕩瑞靄。
"High eaves curl up into the wind,
While palm trees rustle in the mild
air."

故宮新館
New administration
& research block.

聚精英於一堂，採文物於萬古。
"Let the finest talents be assembled in
one hall, The rarest antiquities be selected
from all the ages."

國際人士參與建院六十年紀念大會
International scholars attend the National Palace Museum's 60th anniversary.

内院廣場綠陰滴翠
Greenery and shady
trees in the museum
forecourt.

縱目頂樓無限意，近山疊翠遠山青。
"Rooftops draw the eye onward without end, And green hillsides lead on to distant blue mountains."

飛簷櫛比氣象萬千 （佚名）
Endlessly varied projecting eaves.

深谷樓台淹日月，雙谿遊侶共雲山。

"In the secluded valley, storied buildings weather the passing years. Where two streams flow, wandering companions share the mist-cloaked mountain views."

本院正廳大門入口
The museum's main
entrance foyer.

一樓大廳
The ground floor concourse.

高山仰止，景行行止。
"As one pauses to look up at high mountains, So one pauses in a walk to admire the scene all around."

先總統　蔣公畫像
Portrait of the late President Chiang Kai-shek.

觀古今於須臾，撫四海於一瞬。
（晉　陸機文賦）

"Let us survey all history in a flash, Embrace all lands in the twinkling of an eye." — Lu Chi-wen, Chin Dynasty (265-420)

華夏文化與世界文化之關係展示室之一
Chinese Culture and World Cultures. (1)

懷抱觀古今
華夏文化與世界文化之關係

Comprehensive Insight into the Sweep
of History-
Chinese Culture and World Cultures

華夏文化與世界文化之關係展示室之二
Chinese Culture and World Cultures. (2)

華夏文化與世界文化之關係展示室之三
Chinese Culture and World Cultures. (3)

多媒體幻燈片放映室(二)
Multi-media slides presentation room (2)

多媒體幻燈片放映室(一)
Multi-media slides presentation room (1)

光焜焜而煬耀兮，紛郁郁而暢美。
（後漢書　馮衍傳）
"Shining with fresh lustre, Beauty befitting the odour of incense." — Biography of Feng Yen, *Latter Han History*.

商周　青銅禮器陳列室之一
Shang & Chou bronze ritual vessels (1).

商晚期　　獸面紋貫耳壺
*Hu* with vertical lugs and
animal mask decor, Late
Shang dynasty (ca. 14th-
11th centuries B.C.)

西周晚期　　　頌壺
Sung *Hu*, Late Western
Chou dynasty (ca. 9th-
8th centuries B.C.)

寶鼎見兮色紛縕，煥其鼎兮被龍紋。
（漢　班固賦）

"Gorgeous are the precious *ting* tripods, Patterned all over with motifs of dragons." —
Pan Ku, Latter Han Dynasty (25-220)

商周　青銅禮器陳列室之二
Shang & Chou bronze ritual
vessels (2).

環四海以爲鼎，跨九垠以爲爐。
　　　（唐　柳宗元　貞符序）

"The *ting* tripod reeves in the four seas,
The *lu* incense burner bestrides the nine
provinces." — Liu Tsung-yuan, T'ang
Dynasty (618-907)

商周　青銅禮器陳列室之三
Shang & Chou bronze ritual
vessels (3).

不狩不獵，胡瞻爾庭。
〔詩 魏風〕
"Without chasing and hunting, How will we see game in your courtyard?" — *Classic of Odes,* Chou Dynasty (11th century-256 B.C.)

戰國 狩獵紋壺
*Hu* with hunting scenes, Warring States period (ca. 5th-3rd centuries B.C.)

禮釋回增美質（禮記　禮器）
"Ritual meaning enhances the
beauty of a vessel." — *Li Chi*,
Ritual Vessels section.

西周晚期　頌氏家族器：鼎、壺、簋
Ritual bronzes of the Sung clan, Late
Western Chou Dynasty (11th century
− 771 B.C.)

懷仁饗德 （禮記　禮器）
"Cherish benevolence,
Nourish virtue" — *Li
Ch'i*, Ritual Vessels sec-
tion.

商末周初　諸妘方尊
Ch'u Ssu *Fang-Tsun*,
Late Shang/Early West-
ern Chou dynasties (ca.
11th centuries B.C.)

38

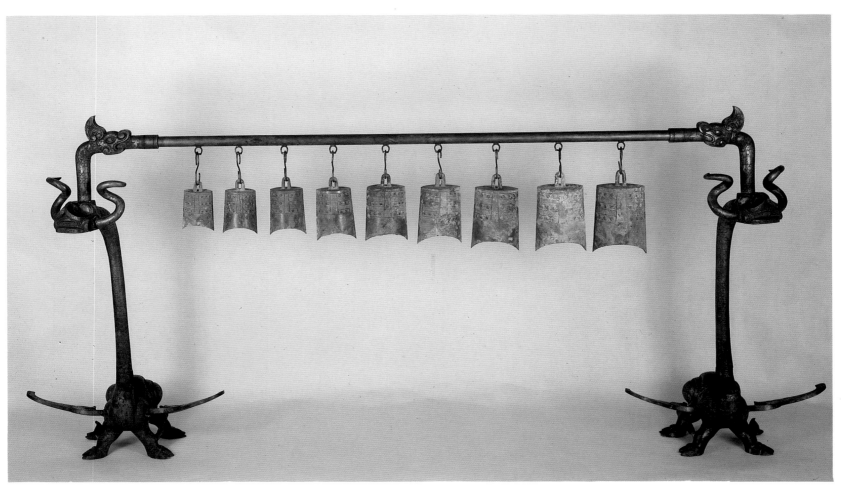

禮以道志，樂和其聲。
　　（禮記　樂記）

"Ritual is based on the True Way, While music joins all voices in harmony" — *Li Chi*, Music section.

春秋中晚期　編鐘

Set of nine *Chung* with interlaced hui-snake decor, hanging on a frame which is a modern reproduction, Middle to Late Spring & Autumn period (ca. 7th-5th centuries B.C.)

樂而無怨，禮至不爭。
（禮記　樂記）

"Music banishes all malcontent, Ritual obviates all envious striving". — Li Chʹi, Music section.

春秋中晚期　編磬

Set of ten stone *Ch'ing* hanging on a frame which is a modern reproduction, Middle to Late Spring & Autumn period (ca. 7th-5th centuries B.C.)

出其尊彝，陳其俎豆。
（國語）

"Let the sacrificial vessels
be brought forth. Let the
altar of sacrifice be laid
out." — *Conversations of
the States.*

西周中期　服方尊
Fu *Fang-Tsun*, Mid-
dle Western Chou-
dynasty (ca. 10th-
9th centuries B.C.)

安國如鼎呂（宋　范成大句）
"May the state exist in harmony. As exampled by the nine *ting* tripods and the Chou imperial bells." — Fan Ch'eng-ta, Sung Dynasty (960-1127)

商周　青銅禮器陳列室之四
Shang & Chou bronze ritual vessels (4).

先王定鼎山河固，寶命乘周萬物新。
（唐　宋之問詩）
"When the former kings designated the *ting* tripod, the state was secure, When the precious mandate was conferred upon Chou, all things became as new ." — Sung Chih-wen, T'ang Dynasty (618-907)

青銅工藝的復興—戰國鑲嵌器陳列櫃
Revival of bronze art-display case with inlaid bronzes of the Warring States period. (475-221 B.C.)

西周中期　師湯父鼎
Shih-T'ang-Fu *Ting*,
Middle Western Chou
dynasty (ca. 10th-9th
centuries B.C.)

西周晚期　鬲叔匜
Fu-Shu *Yi*, Late Western Chou dynasty (ca. 9th-8th centuries B.C.)

商晚期 犧首乳丁紋罍
*Lei* with nipple and ram head decor, Late Shang dynasty (ca. 14th-11th centuries B.C.)

46

商晚期　蟠龍紋盤
*P'an* with coiled
dragon decor, Late
Shang dynasty (ca.
14th-11th centuries
B.C.)

商末周初 方簋
*Fang-Kuei*, Late Shang/
Early Western Chou
dynasties (ca. 11th cen-
tury B.C.)

戰國早期　鳥首獸身尊
*Tsun* in form of a bird-
headed beast, Early War-
ring States period (ca. 5th
century B.C.)

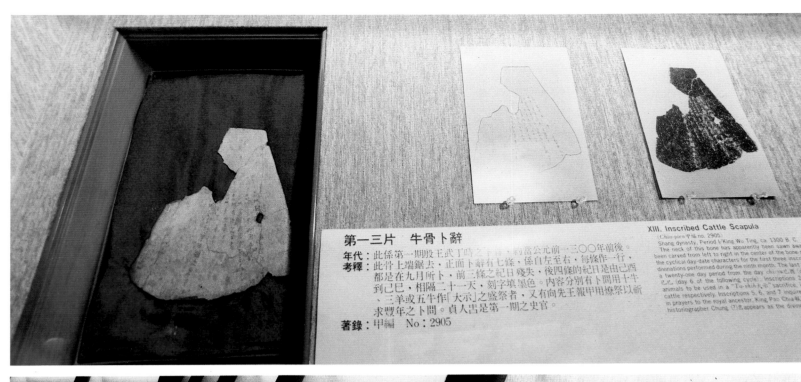

第一三片 牛骨卜辭

年代：此係第一期殷王武丁時之卜骨，約當公元前一三〇〇年前後。
考釋：此骨上端鋸去，正面卜辭有七條，係自左至右，每條作一行，
都是在九月所卜，前三條之紀日殘失，後四條的紀日是由己酉
到己巳，相隔二十一天，刻字填墨色。內容分別有卜問用十牛
三羊或五牛作「大示」之盛祭者，又有向先王報甲用燎祭以祈
求豐年之卜問。貞人愛是第一期之史官。
著錄：甲編 No：2905

### XIII. Inscribed Cattle Scapula
(Chin-pien 甲編 no. 2905)

Shang dynasty, Period I, King Wu Ting, ca 1300 B.C.
The neck of this bone has apparently been sawn away. Seven verti
been carved from left to right in the center of the bone plate and three
the cyclical day-date characters for the first three inscriptions are mis
divinations performed during the ninth month. The last four inscriptio
a twenty-one day period from the day chi-yu 己酉 (day 46 of the
己巳 (day 6 of the following cycle). Inscriptions 2, 3, and 4 in
animals to be used in a "Ta-shih 大示" sacrifice, i.e. ten head
cattle respectively. Inscriptions 5, 6, and 7 inquire about the us
in prayers to the royal ancestor, King Pao Chia 報甲 for an abun
historiographer Chung 愛 appears as the diviner inquiring on

第三片 龜甲卜辭

年代：此係第一期武丁時之卜甲，約當公元前一三〇〇年前後。
考釋：此係甲骨左右各長...

古文明的證言
Testimony of ancient
civilization.

商　甲骨文陳列室
Shang oracle bone
gallery.

三千年前，東亞唯一的通
行文字
甲骨文的世界
（中央研究院歷史語言研究所借展）

East Asia's Only Script Medium 3,000
Years Ago-
The World of Oracle-bone Inscriptions
(Loan Exhibition by The Institue of History and Philology. Academia
Sinica)

質人底事卜靈龜？商湯之民無凍餒。
What need the righteous man resort to divina-
tion?  Under King T'ang, the people of Shang
were free of hunger and cold.''

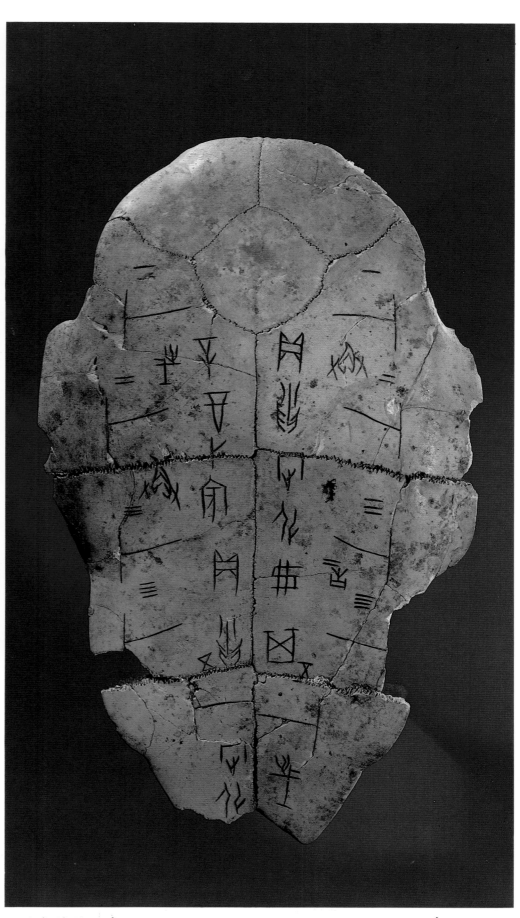

三千年前的紀事
Records of events
from 3,000 years
ago.

商　甲骨文
Oracle Bones, Late
Shang dynasty (ca.
14th-11th centuries
B.C.)

51

守著風，守著霧，我在夜中守著祢。
（民國　商禽詩）

"In rain or in mist, Through the night I keep guard over you." — Shang Ch'in, Republic of China (1911-)

商晚期　大理石虎首人身虎爪形立雕　大理石鴞形立雕

Carved Marble Monster Figure, Carved Marble Owl Figure, Late Shang dynasty (ca. 14th-11th centuries B.C.)

東亞文明的瑰寶
殷墟出土石，骨雕
（中央研究院歷史語言研究所借展）

Treasures of East Asian Civilization-
Stone and Bone Carvings from Shang
Imperial Tombs
(Loan Exhibition by The Institue of History and Philology. Academia
Sinica)

殷墟出土骨塤
Bone musical
instrument from
Shang imperial
tomb.

天之牖民，如壎如篪。
（詩　大雅）
"Heaven's guiding the people
is like an ocarina, like a flute"
— *Classic of Odes*, Chou Dynasty (11th century-256 B.C.)

商晚期　石梟（正面）
Stone owl (front view),
Late Shang dynasty (17
th-11th centuries B.C.)

53

殷墟1001大墓模型
Model of Shang tomb
1001 at Anyang.

商晚期　大理石雕"鳥"面管
（上）正面，（下）側面
Carved marble object with double "bird-mask" decor, Late Shang dynasty (ca. 14th-11th centuries B.C.)

商晚期　石立鴞小立雕
Small carved stone owl figurine, Late Shang dynasty (ca. 14th-11th centuries B.C.)

風廻一鏡揉藍淺，雨過天青潑墨濃。
（耶律楚材詩）

"Flurries of wind ruffle the pale blue mirrorlike pond, But under clear skies when the rain has passed it resumes the thick blackness of ink." — Yeh-lü Ch'u-ts'ai, Yüan Dynasty (1271-1368)

唐　海獸葡萄紋銅鏡
Bronze mirror with lions and grapevine T'ang dynasty (618 907)

鑑古知今
銅鏡陳列室

Seeking the Reflection of Today
in the Past-
Bronze Mirror Gallery

去天之象，則地之靈；
萬物不能逃其跡，百怪不能遁其形。
Its principles are laid down by heavenly phenomena and earthly essences; Nothing escapes
undetected, from it nothing can hide."

唐　三樂鏡
Bronze mirror with Confucius
and Jung Chi- ch'i in conver-
sation, T'ang dynasty.(618- 907)

唐　月宮故事鏡
Flower-shaped bronze mirror
with scene of the Moon Palace, T'ang dynasty (618- 907)

道人胸中水鏡清，萬象起滅逃無形。
（宋　蘇軾詩）

"A just man's heart is clear as a crystal mirror,
The alpha and omega of all phenomena are
reflected there." — Su Shih, Sung Dynasty
(960-1279)

銅鏡展示室
Bronze mirror
gallery.

肝膽誠難隱，妍媸信易窮。
幸居君子室，長願免蒙塵。
　　　　　　（唐　闕名詩）
"True sincerity cannot be long
hidden, but the credit of a superficial
man is soon exhausted. How fortunate that I dwell in your presence,
where I may remain eternally
unsullied." — Anonymous T'ang
Dynasty (618-907)

清 "西清續鑑"（上）與 "寧壽
續鑑"（下）鏡匣 及其所藏銅鏡
"Hsi-Ch'ing hsü-chien" mirror case
(above) and "Ning- Shou hsü-chien"
mirror case (below), Ch'ing dynasty
(1644-1911)

二樓入口門廳
Floor 2 en-
trance foyer.

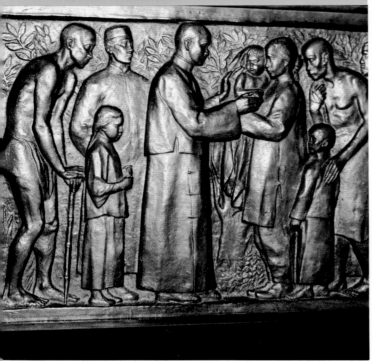

國父與民眾浮雕
Bas-relief showing
Sun Yat-sen with
ordinary Chinese
citizens.

國父 孫中山先生銅像
Bronze statue of Sun Yat-
sen founder of the Republic
of China.

61

二樓巨幅書畫作品陳列櫃
Floor 2 display cases for large paintings and calligraphic works.

西域職貢貽咸寶富籠常見非奇弥珠毛
翠角固可愛邪成雛曾寧聞數歲前乃
盲兩穀雛伏翼之領哺蜀狱滲弱質隨雌
俓老雀籠中情反邀三年大花
下閉屏臺翠毬絆羽暎日嬌輝圓眼凌
風張筒低苑嬾條高屋備萬綬罷咙戎習
籬拷之即末拓之舞那眾絢匈慧跟尖柘
禽六織土產好菁韍杖樣風人藻盞延濟
故禽六織土產好菁韍杖樣風人藻盞延濟
戊寅六月晥望懇懷捂
御筆

清　郎世寧　孔雀開屏圖
Peacocks,　Lang　Shih-ning
(Giuseppe　Castiglione;　1688-
1766),　Ch'ing　dynasty.

63

茫茫造化，二儀既分。
散氣流衍；既陶既甄。
　（晋　張華詩）
"The whole vast creation is
divided between earth and sky;
Its diffuse powers are harnes-
sed by the potter and his
kiln." — Chang Hua, Chin
Dynasty (265-420)

傳統窯業製作展示室
Display of traditional
ceramics manufacture.

景德鎮蛋式窯模型
Model of a Ching-te-
chen eggshell-shaped
kiln.

古登窯窯場模型
Model of a Ku-teng
ware kiln.

是件不朽的記憶，
是件不肯讓消失的努力，
是件想挽回什麼的欲望。
（民國　席慕蓉詩）

"It's an undying memory, It's
an effort not to disappear, The
desire to retrieve something from
the past." — Hsi Mu-jung, Republic of China (1911-)

陶瓷陳列室之一
Porcelain gallery (1)

唐　三彩文官騎馬俑
Triple-colour glazed figurine of a civil official on horseback, T'ang Dynasty (618-907)

先民並杵椎舂，合以丹青之色。
"The ancients pounded with pestle and mortar, Mixing the essences into pigments for painting."

唐　三彩天王俑—增長天
Three-colored pottery image of virudhaka, T'ang dynasty (618-907)

67

瓷器陳列室之二
Porcelain gallery (2)

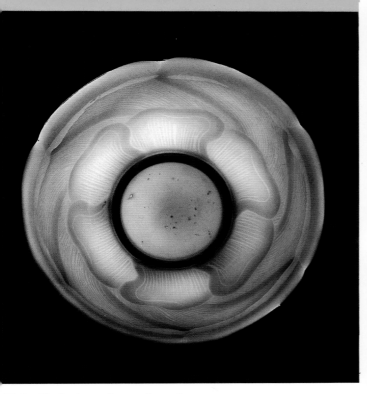

圓似月魂墮，輕如雲魄起。
（唐 皮日休詩）

"Perfectly round, as if the full moon had fallen to earth; Wonderfully light, like frail mist rising heavenwards." — P'i Jih-hsiu, T'ang Dynasty (618-907)

明初　官窯　甜白葵花小盌
Small bowl with incised mallow flower decoration, sweet-white glaze, Early Ming period.

青如天，明如鏡；
薄如紙，聲如磬。（博物要覽）

"Blue as the sky, bright as a mirror; Of paper thinness, with the true tone of a chime." — Po-wu Yao-lan by Ku T'ai, Ming Dynasty (1368-1644)

（上）宋　官窯　月白雙耳三足爐
（下）宋　鈞窯　粉青蓮花式大盌
(above) Tripodal incense burner with two handles, moon white glaze, Kuan ware, Sung dynasty. (960-1279) (below) Lotus-petal large bowl, Chün ware, Sung dynasty (960-1279)

69

尊中永注丁香紫，儀狄當年無此物。
"Clove purple is forever caught in the glaze of this vase; Surely no meaner race ever saw its like."

宋　鈞窯　丁香紫尊
Lilac-glazed jar, *Chün* ware, Sung dynasty (960-1279)

定州花瓷垂龍耳，釉裏蓮花永不謝。
"This Ting-ware porcelain with dragon-shaped loops holds lotuses in its glaze which will never wither."

宋　定窯　牙白劃花蓮花龍耳壺
Jar with dragon-shaped handles and lotus decoration, Ting ware, Sung dynasty (960-1279)

崑山片玉不爲奇，萬目爭看北定瓷。
"What charm can jade from K'un-shan hold,
When all strive only to gaze upon Ting ware
from the north?"

宋瓷陳列室一角
Part of the Sung
porcelain gallery.

宋代名窯瓷器陳列櫃
Display cabinet exhibiting famous Sung porcelain wares.

宋　定窰　牙白劃花蓮花瓶
Vase with lotus decoration,
Ting ware, Sung dynasty (960-
1279)

74

宋　官窯　粉青貫耳穿帶壺
Vase with loop handles, Kuan
ware, Sung dynasty (960-1279)

75

宋　汝窯　粉青奉華紙槌瓶
Paper mallet-shaped vase, Ju
ware, Sung dynasty (960-1279)

宋 哥窯 灰青沖耳乳足爐
Tripodal incense burner with
ring handles, Ko ware, Sung
dynasty (960-1279)

元 景德鎮窯 釉裏紅花卉大碗
Large underglaze red bowl with floral
decoration, Ching-te-chen ware, Yüan
dynasty (1279-1368)

天球瓶上舞青龍
Blue dragons dance on
a vase with a celestial
sphere.

明　永樂窯　青花龍紋天球瓶
Underglaze blue vase with dragon
and lotus decoration, Yung-lo ware,
Ming dynasty (1368-1644)

明　永樂窯 青花花果梅瓶
Vase with flower and fruit
decoration in underglaze blue,
Yung-lo ware, Ming dynasty
(1368-1644)

明　正德窯　天藍地三彩番蓮花盆
Blue-ground flower bowl with Indian
lotus decoration in three-colored glazes,
Cheng-te ware, Ming dynasty (1368-
1644)

明 成化窯 鬥彩花鳥高足盃
Stemcup with birds and flowers
in Tou-ts'ai enamel, Cheng-hua
ware, Ming dynasty (1368-1644)

清 雍正窯 琺瑯彩花蝶茶壺
Teapot with design of flowers
and butterflies in Polychrome
enamel, Yung-cheng ware, Ch'ing
dynasty (1644-1911)

清　康熙窯　宜興胎加彩花卉蓋盌
Covered bowl with Yi-hsing stone ware
body and polychrome enamel with
floral decoration, K'ang-hsi ware,
Ch'ing dynasty (1644-1911)

清　康熙窯　五彩鏤空香薰
Open-work censer with Wu-ts'ai
enamel, K'ang-hsi ware Ch'ing
dynasty (1644-1911)

清　乾隆窯　釉裏紅福壽瓶
Vase with design of bats and
peaches in underglaze red,
Ch'ien-lung ware, Ch'ing dynasty (1644–1911)

浮梁陶藝兼三絕，皆是唐英手中興。
"Porcelain-making demands all-round artistic excellence, And to this T'ang Ying may truly lay just claim."

清　乾隆　官窯瓷器
Kuan-ware porcelain of the Ch'ien-lung period (1736-1795), Ch'ing Dynasty.

聖既希天，賢亦希聖。
（晋　夏侯湛句）
"The Sage yearns to match
Heaven's virtue, While the
virtuous man yearns to rival
the Sage." — Hsia-hou Chan,
Chin Dynasty (265-420)

二樓畫廊書畫陳列櫃
（歷代先聖先賢圖像展）
Exhibition of the Por-
traits of Ancient ages
and sacred Men.

外師造化，中得心源
本院書畫陳列室

Base Outward Forms on Nature,
but Draw Inner Meaning from the
Wellsprings of the Heart-
Painting and Calligraphy Galleries

明　仇英　先賢圖
Ancient Sages, Ch'iu
Ying (ca. 1494-1552),
Ming dynasty.

宋人　却坐圖
Telling the Con-
cubine Where to
sit, Anonymous,
Sung　dynasty
(960-1279)

87

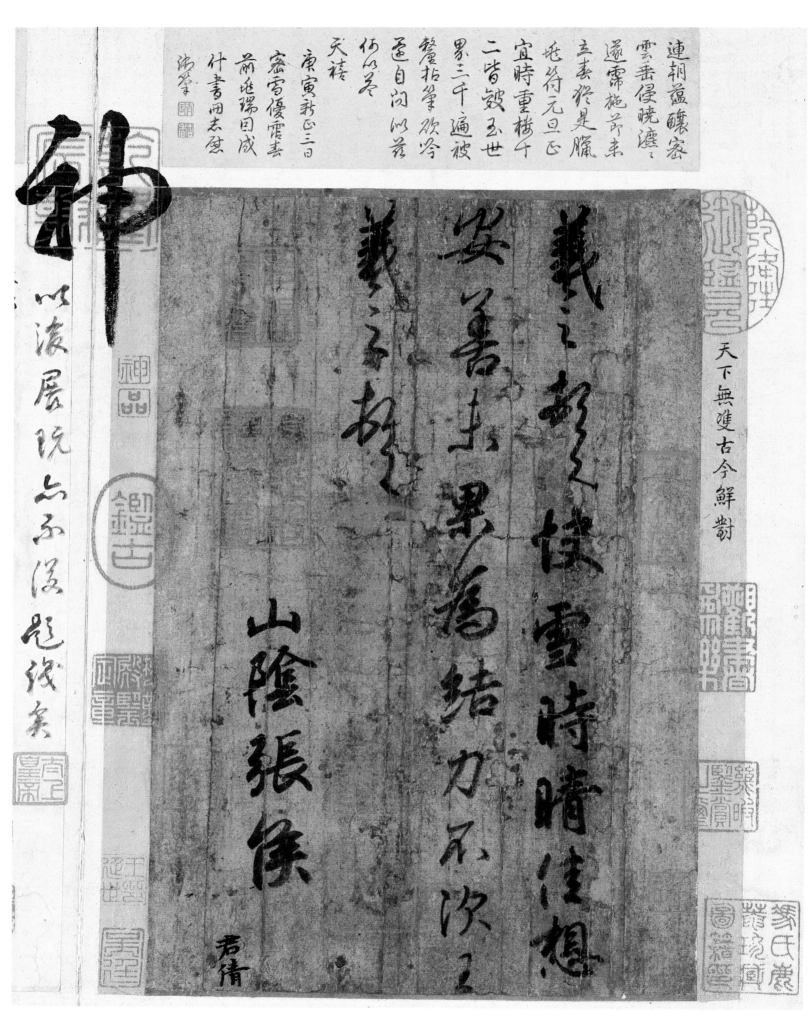

連朝薀釀密
雲垂垂侵曉瀌瀌
遙霜施艻末
立表終是脘
秪符元旦正
宜時重樓千
二皆鼓玉世
累三千遍被
磬拈筆欽岺
遙自閔以善
何以善
天禧
寅寅新正三日
嘉雪優雪去
前延瑞日成
什書册志慰
御筆

天下無雙古今鮮對

以澇屢院不浸飐俊衷

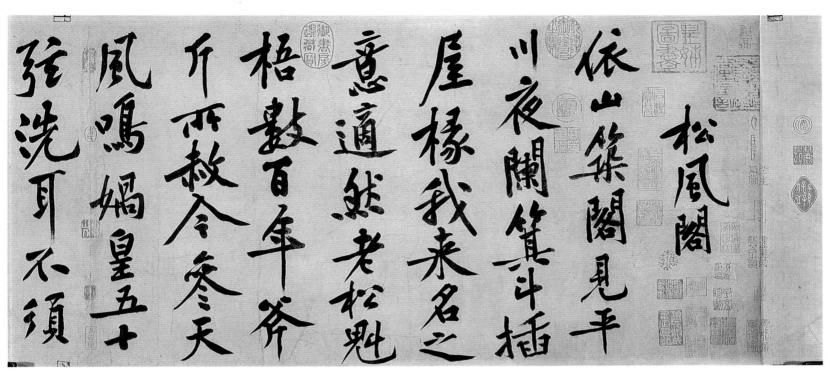

松風閣

依山築閣見平
川夜闌箕斗插
屋椽我来名之
意適然老松魁
梧數百年斧
斤所赦令參天
風鳴媧皇五十
弦洗耳不須

宋 黃庭堅 松風閣詩（局部）
Poem of the Hall of Pines and
Wind, (detail) Huang T'ing-chien
(1045-1105), Sung dynasty.

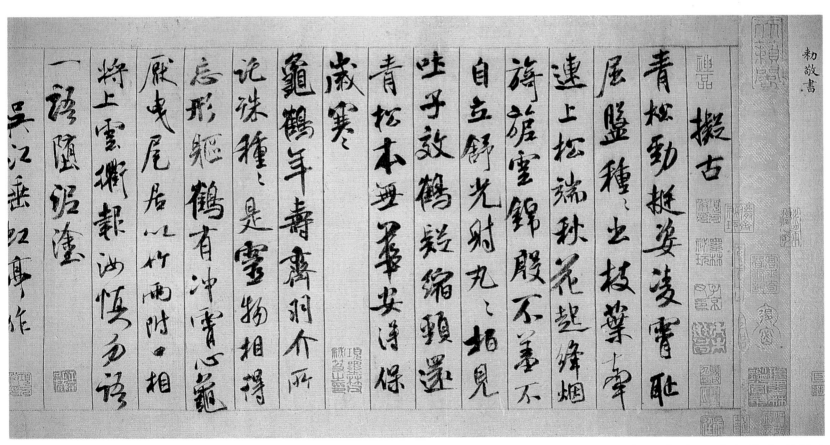

擬古

青松勁挺姿凌霄恥
屈監種、出枝葉十尋
連上松端秋花起絳煙
蔣莚垒錦殿不羞不
自立舒光射丸、相見
吐子效鶴舂縮頸還
青松本無華安浮保
歲寒、
龜鶴年壽齊羽介所
記珠種、是靈物相持
厭戈尾居以竹雨附口相
忘形粗鶴有沖霄心籠
將上雲衢報汕慎而五語
一語隨沿塗
吳江乘虹再作

宋 米芾 蜀素帖（局部）
Calligraphy on Szechuan silk,
(detail) Mi Fei (1051-1107),
Sung dynasty.

89

細展千緗日已昏，靜觀萬物春長在。
"How quickly the day passes in scrutinizing
fine paintings; Placidly viewing the variety
of nature truly contents the heart."

書畫 册頁 手卷 陳列室
Gallery displaying album-
leaves and handscrolls of
painting and calligraphy.

元　黃公望　富春山居圖（局部）
Dwelling in the Fu-Ch'un Mountain,
(detail) Huang-Kung-wang (1268-1354)
Yüan dynasty.

身雖在花溪，垂綸看今古。
"Although afar off on banks of
blossom-lined stream, True insight
into history may be gained while
dangling one's line."

明　唐寅　溪山漁隱圖（局部）
Hermit Anglers on a Mountain
Stream, (detail) T'ang Yin (1470-
1523) Ming dynasty.

寄詩情於畫外，開風氣不爲師。
"Let your painting subtly suggest poetic images, Be bold and free, not beholden to exemplars."

五代　秋林羣鹿
Herd of Deer in an Autumnal Grove, Anonymous, Five dynasties(906-960)

此中大有消遙處，難說與君畫與君。
（明　唐寅詩）
"Here a great spirit of freedom moves, No knowing what other master can match your painting." — T'ang Yin, Ming Dynasty (1368-1644)

明　陳洪綬　蓮池應化圖
Buddha Incarnated as the
Patriarch Lien-chih, Ch'en
Hung-shou (1599-1652),
Ming dynasty.

宋　黄居寀　山鷓棘雀圖
Pheasant and Thorny Shrubs,
Hang Chu-t'sai, (933-993),
Sung dynasty.

揮灑自如，筆有江山之助。
"Natural and unpretentious, The artist's brush is impelled by noble scenes."

歷代書畫展覽
Annual Special Exhibition of Treasured Paintings and Calligraphic Works.

彡毫妙處見童心

"In triumphs of the
inted brush One spies
he artist's childlike
urity of heart."

宋人 冬日嬰戲圖（局部）
Children Playing on a Winter
Day, (detail) Anonymous,
Sung dynasty (960-1279)

95

唐人　宮樂圖
Palace Musicians,
Anonymous, T'ang
dynasty (618-907)

宋　李唐　萬壑松風圖
Soughing Wind among
Mountain Pines, Li Ta'ng
(1049-1130), Sung dyn-
asty.

宋　范　寬　谿山行旅圖
Travelers among Mountain
and Stream, Fan K'uan
(early 11th century), Sung
dynasty.

99

宋繡　咸池浴日圖
Sun Rising over a Turbulent
Sea, embroidery, Sung dynasty

宋　沈子蕃　緙絲山水圖
Landscape, silk tapestry,
Shen Tzu-fan, Sung dynasty
(960-1279)

花含天地笑，鳥為古今呼。
"Flowers laugh for joy of all creation, Birds sing the truth of every century."

明　呂紀　秋鷺芙蓉圖
Egrets and Hibiscus in Autumn, Lu Chi (1477-?), Ming dynasty.

明　沈周　廬山高圖
Lofty Mount Lu, Shen
Chou (1427-1509), Ming
dynasty

清　石溪　山高水長圖
High Mountain and Long
Streams K'un Ts'an (1612-
ca. 1673), Ch'ing dynasty.

玉器陳列室一角
Part of the jade
gallery.

光彩流映，氣如虹霞 。
君子是佩，象德閑邪 。
（晉　郭璞詩）

Lustrous in its radiant
sheen, shot through like
evening clouds; To wear
this is a symbol of virtue
and a shield against all
harm." — Kuo P'u, Chin
Dynasty (265-420)

戰國　玉戚
*Ch'i*, ceremonial jade
battle axe, Warring
States period (ca. 5th-
3rd centuries B.C.)

105

新石器時代晚期—商前期 玉圭陳列櫃
*Kuei*, ceremonial jade tablet, Late neolithic period to early Shang dynasty (ca. 23rd-14th centuries B.C.)

新石器時代晚期—商前期　鳥紋圭
*Kuei*, ceremonial jade tablet, Late neolthic period to early Shang dynasty (ca. 23rd-14th centuries B.C.)

皎皎無瑕玷，鎗鎗有佩聲 。
（唐　辛洪詩）

"Gloriously and immaculately pure,
Jade pendants tinkle as you walk." —
Hsing Hung, T'ang Dynasty (618-
907)

商　鳥紋珮
Jade pendant
in the bird
motif, Shang
dynasty (ca.
16th-11th cen-
turies B.C.)

新石器時代中晚期　素璧

*Pi*, ceremonial jade dise, Middle to late neolithic period (ca. 35th-18th centuries B.C.)

戰國　穀紋璜
*Huang,* ceremonial jade with grain pattern, Warring States period (ca. 5th-3rd centuries B.C.)

漢　玉辟邪
*Pi-hsieh,* jade winged beast, Han
dynasty (206B.C.-220A.D.)

戰國　瓏
*Lung,* ceremonial jade in the
shape of a dragon, Warring States
period (ca. 5th-3rd centuries B.C.)

新石器時代中晚期　琮
*T'sung,* ceremonial jade tube, Middle to late neolithic period (ca. 35th-18th centuries B.C.)

商 琮

*T'sung*, ceremonial
jade tube, Shang
dynasty (ca. 16th-
11th centuries B.C.)

113

只留下隔玻璃這奇蹟難信，
猶帶著后土依依的祝福。
（民國　余光中詩）
"Just beyond the glass lies a miracle
most wonderful, Still clothed in
Mother Earth's first benediction." —
Yü Kuang-chung, Republic of China
(1911-)

宋　黄玉荷葉　筆洗
Brownish yellow jade
brush—washer in the
shape of a lotus leaf,
Sung dynasty (960-
1279)

故人似玉由來重 （唐 李太白詩）
"True friends have the sterling weight of jade." — Li Po, T'ang Dynasty (618-907)

宋　白玉角形觥
White jade vessel in the shape of an animal's horn, Sung dynasty (960-1279)

有色同寒冰，無物隔纖塵。
（唐　羅維詩）
"It has the colour of cool ice, But the purity of an insubstantial essence." — Lo Wei, T'ang Dynasty (618-907).

玉器陳列室一角
Part of the jade gallery.

清　瑪瑙帶鈎

Agate belt hook
Ch'ing dynasty (A.D.1644 – 1911)

清　紅玉髓瑙桃莩洗
Carnelian brush washer with peach
and bat decoration
Ch'ing dynasty (A.D.1644 – 1911)

清　瑪瑙佛手筆洗

Agate brush washer in the shape of
a bergamot
Ch'ing dynasty (A.D.1644 – 1911)

映物隨顏色，倉空無表裏。
（唐　韋應物詩）
"It reflects the colour of whatever
it lies near. With all the impartiality
of the wide blue sky." — Wei Ying-
wu, T'ang Dynasty (618-907)

清　瑪瑙器陳列櫃
Ch'ing Dynasty agate
gallery.

漢　玉蟬　（六　件）
*Ch'an* Jade cicada (six pieces),
Han dynasty (206B.C.-220A.D.)

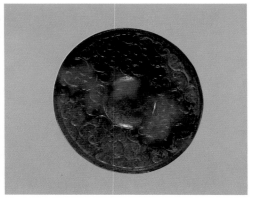

漢　玉劍首　（二件）

*Chien-shou*, Jade pommel of
a sword (two pieces), Han
dynasty (206B.C.-220A.D.)

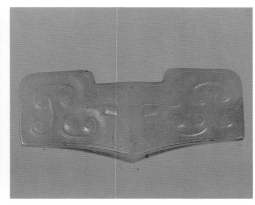

漢　玉璲　（二　件）

*Peng*, jade guard of a sword
(two pieces), Han dynasty (206
B.C.-220A.D.)

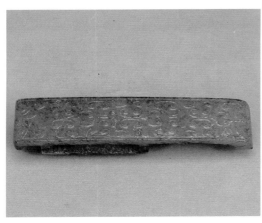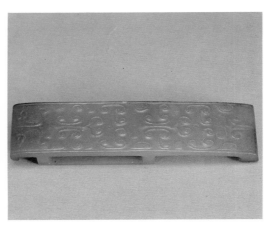

漢　玉璏　（二　件）

*Wei,* jade scabbard buckle (two pieces), Han dynasty (206B.C.-220A.D.)

漢　玉珌　（二　件）

*Pi,* jade chape of scabbard (two pieces), Han dynasty (206 B.C.-220A.D.)

淡煙流水畫屏幽 （宋　秦觀句）
"Pale mists and flowing streams Lend
quiet grace to this painted screen." —
Ch'in Kuan, Sung Dynasty (960-1279)

清　碧玉屏風
Wooden screen inlaied
with green jade plates,
Ch'ing dynasty (1644-
1911)

121

清　翠玉雕刻陳列櫃
Display cabinet exhibiting Ch'ing dynasty carved jadeite.

122

中有美璞凝寒晶，
唯有鬼工能琢成。
（元　張翥詩）

"The icy crystals of this fine raw jade, Await the master craftsman's unique skill." — Chang Chu, Yüan Dynasty (1271-1368)

清　翠玉白菜
Jadeite cabbage,
Ch'ing dynasty
(1644-1911)

陳設類玉器陳列櫃
Decorative jades gallery.

清 碧玉 鰲魚花插
Green jade flower con-
tainer shaped as a pair
of fish-dragon, Ch'ing
dynasty (1644-1911)

明 白玉 鰲魚花插
White jade flower con-
tainer in the shape of
fish-dragon, Ming dy-
nasty (1368-1644)

清 皇室服飾（朝珠、腰飾、腰帶）
Ch'ing imperial clothing and accessories (court necklaces, belts ornaments and belts).

玉梳鈿朵香膠解，盡日風吹玳瑁箏。
（唐　元稹詩）

"Perfumed airs waft from hairpins and combs
of jade, All day long the breezes play through
strands of tortoiseshell." — Yüan Chen, T'ang
Dynasty (618-907)

珠鈿飄起紫霞佩，釵鳳飛來金步搖。
"Hairpins of pearl flash above tawny pendants,
Phoenix tiaras sway with each delicate step."

127

清　皇貴妃冬朝冠
Imperial consort's winter
court crown, Ch'ing dy-
nasty (1644-1911)

清　點翠嵌珠寶囍字鈿子
"Double happiness" hairpin
inlaid with green jade and
pearls, Ch'ing dynasty
(1644-1911)

清　雕黄楊木　西園雅集筆筒
Boxwood brush-holder with a
scene of a gathering of literati,
Ch'ing dynasty (1644-1911)

130

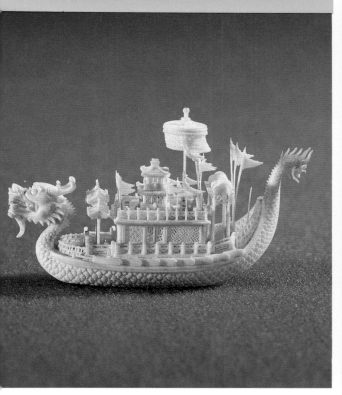

清　雕象牙　龍舟
Ivory dragon-boat,
Ch'ing dynasty (1644-
1911)

清　雕象牙　透花雲龍紋套球
Set of concentric ivory balls
with cloud-dragons in openwork
relief, Ch'ing dynasty (1644-
1911)

清　陳祖章　雕橄欖核舟
（底刻“後赤壁賦”全文）

Olive stone miniature boat
with the Latter Ode on the
Red Cliff carved on its bottom
by Chen Tzu-chang, Ch'ing
dynasty (1644-1911)

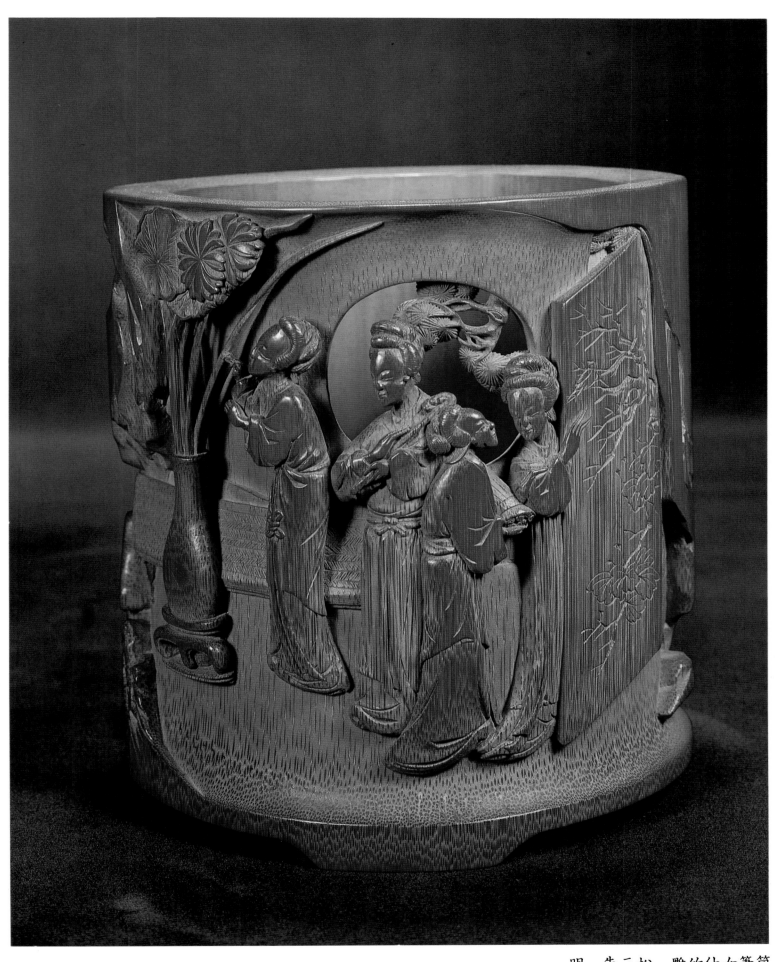

明　朱三松　雕竹仕女筆筒
Carved bamboo brush-holder
with female figures motif by
Chu San-sung, Ming dynasty
(1368-1644)

清　乾隆　仿古雕犀角羣眞海會杯
Rhinoceros horn cup with carving picturing a gathering of Immortals, Ch'ien-lung period (1736-1795), Ch'ing dynasty.

清　雕象牙　四層透花提食盒
Ivory four-tiered food container in openwork relief, Ch'ing dynasty (1644-1911)

明　永樂　剔紅花卉圓盒
Round carved red lacquer box with floral decor, Yung-lo period (1403-1424), Ming dynasty.

# 樹脂的發現
## 圓潤精美的漆器工藝

Discovering the Possibilities
of Resin-
The Gorgeous Intricacy of
Lacquer Ware

清　金漆夾紵大士像
Fabric-core gold-lacqure
image of Avalokitesvara
made in Fu-chou, Ch'ing
dynasty. (1644-1911)

清　剔紅赤壁圖插屏
Carved red lacquer
screen with a scene
from the "Ode on the
Red Cliff", Ch'ing
dynasty (1644-1911)

明　嘉靖　剔彩九龍圓盤
Round carved polychrome
lacquer plate with nine
dragons, Chia-Ch'ing period
(1522-1566), Ming dynasty.

明　宣德款　掐絲琺瑯螭耳洗
Cloisonne basin with hornless-
dragon handles and Hsüan-te reign
mark, Ming dynasty (1368-1644).

明　萬曆款　掐絲琺瑯雙龍盤
Cloisonne plate with paired dragon decore, Wan-li period (1573-1620), Ming dynasty.

明　永樂款　剔紅花卉錐把壺
Carved red lacquer vase with floral decor, Yung-lo period (1403-1424), Ming dynasty.

清　乾隆款　內填琺瑯嵌寶高足蓋盌
Champleve covered high-stem bowls inlaid
with precious stones, Ch'ien-lung period
(1736-1795), Ch'ing dynasty.

明　景泰款　掐絲琺瑯三羊尊
Cloisonne Tsun-vessel with three
goat heads and Ching-tái reign
mark, Ming dynasty (1368-1644)

清　碧玉番蓮花方盒
（附各式珍玩23件）

Square green-jade curio-box with carved India-lotus decor: containing 23 curios, Ch'ing dynasty (1644-1911)

## 珍奇薈萃
## 巧不可諧的多寶格

## Collages of Precious Curios-
## The Inexhaustible Fascination
## of Curio Cabinets

清　竹絲纏枝番蓮花多寶格
Curio cabinet of bamboo and silk with design of intertwined lotus flowers, Ch'ing dynasty (1644-1911).

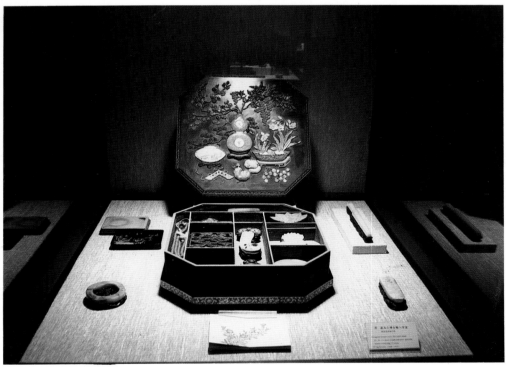

清　嵌玉石博古圖八方盒
（附各式珍玩15件）
Octagonal lacquer curio-box with inlaid Po-ku-t'u decor of jade and semi-precious stones, containing 15 curios, Ch'ing dynasty (1644-1911)

清　竹絲纏枝番蓮花多寶格
（附各式珍玩27件）
Round miniature curio-box with
bamboo strip veneer and twined
India-lotus decor, containing 27
curios, Ch'ing dynasty (1644-
1911)

147

創新，再創新， 而止於至善之境。
"Seek renewal and yet further renewal, Only
stopping when perfection is reached."

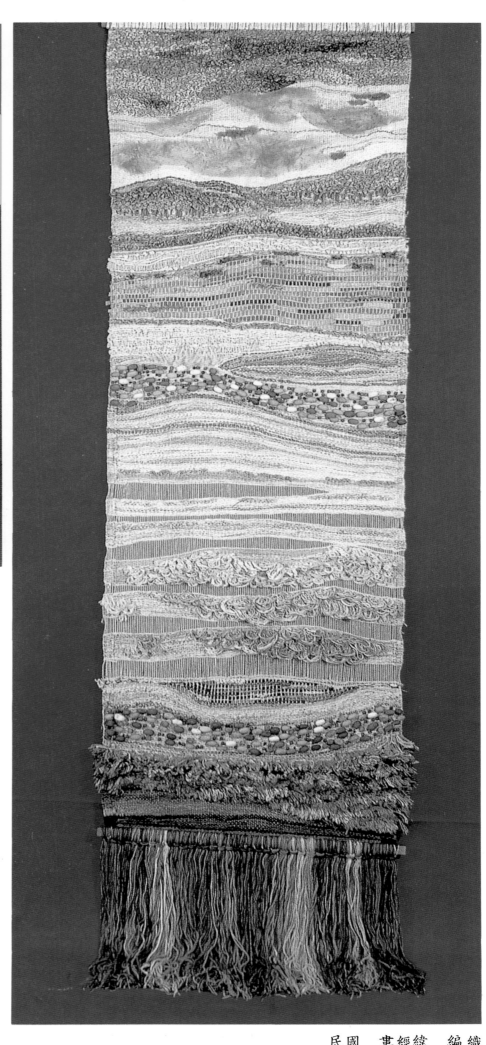

民國　婁經緯　編織
Weaving by Lou Ching-
wei, Republic of China.
(1911-)

149

近代文物陳列室
Contemporary art gallery.

民國　詹鏐淼　皮塑　竹林七賢

"The Seven Sages of the Bamboo Grove", leather sculpture by Chan Liu-miao, Republic of China (1911-)

集顏謝於一堂，領豪素於百代。
"Bring the poets Yen and Hsieh together
in one room, Lead the noblest spirits
of the age."

民國　詹鏐淼　皮塑　竹林七賢
"The Seven Sages of the Bamboo
Grove", leather sculpture by Chan
Liu-miao, Republic of China (1911-)

民國　朱銘　木雕　公孫大娘舞劍器
"The Sword Dance of Kung-sun Ta-niang"
sculpture in wood by Chu Ming, Republic
of China (1911-)

152

民國　孫超　結晶釉瓶
Vase with crystalline glaze,
by Sun Cháo, Republic of
China (1911-)

153

集顏謝於一堂，領豪素於百代。
"Bring the poets Yen and Hsieh together in one room, Lead the noblest spirits of the age."

鳥幽聲忽斷，茶好味重廻。
（唐　齊己詩）
"A bird's distant call dies on the
sudden; The fine aroma of tea
rises once more" — Ch'i Chi, T'ang
Dynasty (618-907)

四樓三希堂古典茶藝
Tea-drinking the tradition-
al Chinese way in the
San Hsi T'ang tearoom,
Floor 4.

黃卷至今眞味在，莫將糟粕待前人。
（金　周昂詩）

"Authentic yellowing scrolls surviving into
our day Remind us not to cast aside the memory
of things past." — Chou Ang, Chin Dynasty
(1115-1234).

珍藏書畫庫房
Storage vaults
for paintings
and calligraphy.

## 精華盡薈
## 故宮寶藏庫房

Definitive Collection of the Finest
in Chinese Art-
The Storage Vaults of the National
Palace Museum

地脈有靈開作隧；
寶箱無恙疊如城。

"Tunnels burrow deep
into the hillside, Safely
storing their treasures
in boxes piled high."

千篇千古在，一詠一驚魂。
（唐 齊己詩）

"A thousand scrolls kept for a
thousand years, Each one holds
infinite delight in store." — Ch'i
Chi, T'ang Dynasty (618-907)

書畫新庫房
New storage vault
for paintings and
calligraphy.

肴饌百家，牙籤壓架；
笙簧六籍，玉軸連雲。
"A rich feast of authors,
ivory book-tags line the
shelves; Sweet harmony of
the classics, jade rollers reach
up to the ceiling."

圖書文獻新庫
New storage vau
for books an
documents.

158

新庫落成新氣象，吉金古篆颺青煙。
"Completion of the new vault opens new horizons, Blue incense wreathes the mystic bronzes and their age-old inscriptions."

銅器新庫房
New storage vault for bronze vessels.

正館大樓 (53年6月開工54年10月完工)
Main museum building
(built in June 1964 – October 1965)

正館大樓 (53年6月開工54年10月完工)
Main museum building
(built in June 1964 – October 1965)

第一次擴建 (55年12月開工56年10月完工)
First stage of expansion
(built in December 1966 – October 1967)

第二次擴建 (58年4月開工59年2月完工)
Second stage of expansion
(built in April 1969 – February 1970)

物外寄遊心，不如升堂窺其奧也。
"Rest not your curious gaze on outward show, But boldly enter and espy the truth within."

行政大樓 (71年9月開工73年3月完工)
Administration block
(built in September 1982 – March 1984)

# 故宮的成長
## 四次擴建工程的回顧

## The Growth of the National Palace Museum— Four Stages of Expansion

莫使紛紅駭綠，亂人心目！
"Oh that brilliant reds and startling greens may not overwhelm these innocent hearts of ours!"

後樂園一角
Part of the
rear garden.

## 古意盎然的
## 後樂園

## Quaint Charm of the Rear Garden

後樂園小徑
Footpath of the rear garden.

萬樹綠低迷，一庭紅撲簌。
（五代 佚名詞）
"All summer, one vast tangle of a myriad green boughs; Come autumn, rustling red leaves carpet all the lawn." — Anonymous, Five Dynasties period (907-960)

後樂園古木
Old trees of the rear garden.

重覓幽香，已入小窗橫幅。
　　　（宋　姜白石詞）
"My search for the source of this sweet fragrance, has led me to this window in the garden wall." — Chiang Pai-shih, Sung Dynasty (960-1279)

傳統風格的至善園門
Traditional Chinese gateway to the Chih-shan Garden.

164

發古幽情
至善園遊踪

Discovering the Tranquillity of
Bygone Days-
A Walk Through the Chin-shan
Sung Dynasty Garden

藻鶴
Artificial cranes

疏欄曲徑遊蹤，綠陰細草清風。
名園如畫，曉日輕煙雅客；何須萬紫千紅？
"Balustraded pathways invite the wanderer; Cool shadows
lie along the soft green grass." "Dawn mists entrance
the visitor to this charming bower; What need pavilions,
red parapets or towers?"

至善園一角
Part of the
Chin-Shan
garden.

165

松竹幽蘭徑，清泉湧坐隅。
　　　　（唐　錢起詩）

'Wild orchids line the path through pine wood and bamboo; Where clear spring bubble here's the place to sit and rest.'' —Ch'ien Ch'i, T'ang Dynasty (618-907)

青山隱隱，綠水漫漫，曲橋涵影，高閣藏煙。
花木鬥錦，幽徑含歡。飛簷之外，白日青天。
"Blue hills in the distance beyond green streams, quaint
bridges cast shadows, tall galleries trap mist. Flowers vie
in gaudy show, quiet pathways beckon; Graceful eaves extend,
a bright flag bravely flutters."

花木扶疏的至善園
The pleasant flowers
and greenery of the
Chih-shan Garden.

167

曲欄杆外天如水（宋　晏殊詩）
"Viewed against angular balustrades, The
sky looks like a sheet of water." — Yen
Shu, Sung Dynasty (960-1279)

至善園仰首翹望的太湖石
Towering ornamental rocks
in the Chih-shan Garden.

山爲翠浪湧，水作玉虹流。
（宋　蘇東坡詩）

"Mountains surge like green billows,
Streams flow like iridescent jade."
— Su Tung-p'o, Sung Dynasty
(960-1279)

至善園碧橋西水榭
Streamside pavilion
by the green bridge
in the Chin-shan
Garden.

百般紅紫鬪芳菲 （唐　韓愈詩）
"In lovely profusion, the flowers contend in fragrant beauty." — Han Yü, T'ang Dynasty (618-907)

洗筆池畔杜鵑開
Azaleas in flower beside the Brush-washing Pond.

入門靄已綠，水禽鳴春塘。
（唐　韋應物詩）
"The light within this bower looks green, And water-fowl chatter on the lake in spring." — Wei Ying-wu, T'ang Dynasty (618-907)

碧橋西水榭一角
Part of the waterside pavilion beside the green bridge.

房屋佔山色，處處兮泉聲。
（唐　錢起詩）
"In dwellings planted amid mountain views, Everywhere, the sound of rushing streams is heard." — Ch'ien Ch'i, T'ang Dynasty (618-907)

碧橋西水榭悠遊的黑天鵝
Graceful black swans by
the waterside pavilion near
the green bridge.

閣外一隅花似錦，階前遍地草如茵。
"There beyond the terrace, flowers bloom
like gaudy chintz; Soft lawns of grass run green
to the every door."

談笑鳳凰花亦笑，天鵝紅掌撥清波。
"Where phoenixes twitter, the flowers also are merry; And the swan's red feet swirl through green wavelets."

松風閣一隅松風閣前洗筆池
View of the "Wind in the Pines Pavilion", with the Brush-washing Lake in front.

手中飛黑電，象外瀉元泉 。
　　　　　　（唐　孟郊詩）
"The inky brush flies like lightning
in the hand, Conjuring nature's vital
forces in its tracery."

松風閣上名家法書刻帖及琴座
Carved example of famous calligraphy and a zither stand in
the "Wind in the Pines Pavilion".

爲物隨指顧，三光爲廻光 。
"All nature follows the Sage's command, sun, moon and stars shine with reflected light."

宋　黃庭堅〝松風閣帖〞原跡之刻石
Stone-carved copy of the "Wind in the Pines Pavilion" calligraphy by Huang T'ing-chien, Sung dynasty (960-1279)

177

晴山看不厭，流水趣何長。
（唐　錢起詩）

"Tirelessly pleasing, the mountains in sparkling sunshine; Endlessly thought-provoking, the bubbling brook flowing along." — Ch'ien Ch'i, T'ang Dynasty (618-907)

松風閣上憑欄遠眺

Looking out from the balustrade of the "Wind in the Pines Pavilion".

泉壑凝神處，陽和布澤時 。
（唐 錢起詩）
"Pausing by this valley brook, One feels the grateful warmth of summer all around." — Ch'ien Ch'i, T'ang Dynasty (618-907)

松風閣外的清溪
The clear stream alongside " the Wing in the Pines Pavilion ".

意將劃地成幽沼，勢擬趨山近小樓。
（唐　秦韜玉詩）

"Here I would like to site my private lake,
Then chivy those tall peaks a little nearer
to my home." --Ch'in T'ao-yü, T'ang Dynasty
(618-907)

蘭亭
Orchid Pavilion.

紅塵飄不到，時有水禽啼 。
　　　　　　（唐　裴度詩）

"No worldly noise is wafted here. Only
the moorhen's ceaseless cackle." — P'ei
Tu, T'ang Dynasty (618-907)

流觴曲水
Stream of Floating Goblets.

傷懷最是雙溪水，日夜長流向海天。
"All my griefs are borne on the double stream below, Which flows night and day down to the open sea."

摩耶精舍大門
Entrance to Chang Ta-ch'ien's residence

亮節高風
張大千紀念館

Conspicuous Virtue and Lofty
Nobility-
The Chang Ta-ch'ien Memorial
House

影娥池
Ying-e Pond.

摩耶精舍中庭
Central courtyard of Chang
Ta-ch'ien's residence.

183

圖從莫窟探神筆，夢遠匡廬寫蜀箋。

"Artistry subime once culled from Tun-huang's
temple walls; Dreams of Szechwan yet haunt
his clifftop studio."

大千先生蠟像

Wax statue of
Chang Ta-ch'ien.

影娥池傍的荷花
Water-lilies beside the
Ying-e Pond.

中庭魚池中的錦鯉
Decorative carp in the
fishpond in the central
courtyard.

摩耶精舍　名貴盆栽 — 古柏
A rare miniature cypress from
Chang Ta-ch'ien's residence.

中庭稀有植物 — 葫蘆竹
A rare calabash bamboo
in the central courtyard
of Chang Ta-ch'ien's.

青松閱世風霜古，翠竹長春雨露新。
"The evergreen pine has known many frosts
and storms, The young bamboo gains freshness
from the dew and rain."

名貴盆栽—連理杜鵑
A rare azalea with link-
ed branches.

鶴林連理花如錦，風露長懷地有情。
"Cranes linger here where flowers bloom like chintz, Through storms and dews my linked boughs show earth's tender care."

在地願爲連理枝—連理杜鵑
A rare azalea with linked
branches, from Chang Ta-
ch'ien's residence.

189

獨自成千古，悠然寄一丘。
潛心於萬物之中，寄與六情之外。
"Alone he rose to timeless fame, Dwelling in this one beloved spot." "Immersed in nature's fold, My heart is free from care."

碧岫觀中人似鶴
"Lost in contemplation of
these green hills, One seems
to grow motionless as a
crane."

後院的仙鶴
Crane of longevity in the
back graden of Chang Ta-
ch'ien's residence.

版權所有

中華民國七十六年元月初版
中華民國七十九年五月再版
中華民國新聞局登記證局版臺業字第2621號

# 故宮勝槩

發 行 人：秦　　孝　　儀
主　　編：袁　　德　　星
攝　　影：董　　　　敏
　　　　　林　傑　人　・　崔　學　國
詩文輯錄：張　曉　風　・　林　恭　祖
出 版 者：國　立　故　宮　博　物　院
　　　　　中華民國臺北市士林區外雙溪
　　　　　電話：（02）8812021-4
　　　　　劃撥帳戶：0012874-1 號
印 刷 者：裕 台 公 司 中 華 印 刷 廠
　　　　　臺北縣新店市寶強路6號
　　　　　電話：（02）9110110-6

Copyright © 1987 by the National Palace Museum
First printing, January 1987
Second printing, May 1990

## THE NATIONAL PALACE MUSEUM
## IN PHOTOGRAPHS

**Publisher:** National Palace Museum
Wai-shuang-hsi, Shih-lin, Taipei 11102, Taiwan
Republic of China

**Printer:** China Art Printing Works Yu-Tai Industrial Corp., Ltd.
6, Pao-chiang Rd., Hsintien 23109, Taipei Taiwan
Republic of China

ISBN 957-562-026-7